By the same author

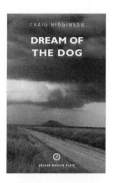

"One of the most perfect one act plays I've seen in ages"
The Independent ****

"engrossing South African drama"
Sunday Times **** (Play of the week)

"One of the best post-Apartheid new dramas we've seen in London"
What's on Stage ****

"this look at black and white South Africans in flux comes painted in remarkably lifelike shades of grey"
The Times ****

"there are two shows you need to see in London: Stoppard's *The Real Thing* and Higginson's *Dream of the Dog*"
Observer ****

"Higginson's intense and involving play"
The Stage

"Higginson's well crafted script of 90 gripping minutes… is both an allegory of Apartheid South Africa and a moving story in its own right"
British Theatre Guide

Craig Higginson

THE GIRL IN THE YELLOW DRESS

OBERON BOOKS
LONDON

First published in 2010 by Oberon Books Ltd
521 Caledonian Road, London N7 9RH
Tel: 020 7607 3637 / Fax: 020 7607 3629
e-mail: info@oberonbooks.com
www.oberonbooks.com

A catalogue record for this book is available from the British Library.

ISBN: 978-1-84943-082-1

Cover photograph designed by Eric Gibson

Printed in Great Britain by CPI Antony Rowe, Chippenham.

For Leila and Phoebe, Amelia and Jack

The Girl in the Yellow Dress was a co-production between Market Theatre, Johannesburg, Live Theatre, Newcastle and Citizens Theatre, Glasgow.

It was first performed at the Grahamstown Festival on 21 June 2010. It then transferred to the Baxter Theatre in Cape Town, the Traverse in Edinburgh, Live Theatre in Newcastle, the Citizens in Glasgow, the Stadsteater in Stockholm and the Market Theatre in Johannesburg.

Cast

CELIA, Marianne Oldham
PIERRE, Nat Ramabulana

Creative Team

Director Malcolm Purkey
Designer Gary McCann
Lighting Designer Nomvula Molepo
Production Manager Drummond Orr
Stage Manager Emelda Khola.

Craig Higginson would like to thank all the theatres and festivals who supported the first run of this play before we had rehearsed it. He is indebted to Gez Casey, Leila Henriques, Jeremy Herrin, Malcolm Purkey, Jeremy Raison and Max Roberts for their brilliant feedback on the various drafts. Craig would also like to thank everyone at Oberon Books and PFD for their constant enthusiasm and support, especially Jessica Cooper, Michael Foster, James Illman, Marie-Therese Lichtenstein and Andrew Walby.

Characters

CELIA

PIERRE

The action takes place in contemporary Paris.
There is no interval.

Part One

THE PASSIVE

CELIA's apartment. Her sitting-room is modern and impeccable, giving a suggestion of wealth. The bookshelves are filled with books. On a mantelpiece, there's a vase filled with daffodils. A half-visible kitchen adjoins the sitting-room. There are also entrances from the front door and CELIA's bedroom.

CELIA's mobile phone is on a glass table. It buzzes like an angry bee.

CELIA emerges from the bedroom. She has just had a shower and is still getting ready. Perhaps she is brushing her hair. She is in her late twenties, pale and beautiful.

She ignores the phone and moves through to the kitchen area to prepare a coffee tray. The phone stops buzzing. Then it beeps.

The doorbell rings. CELIA goes to the door.

CELIA: Hello?

PIERRE: Hello.

CELIA: Are you Pierre?

PIERRE: I am him.

CELIA: Then you'd better come in.

> *PIERRE enters. He is French-speaking. Of African heritage. About twenty. He has dreadlocks and wears a dark blue polar neck jumper. While CELIA closes the door behind him, he regards the books.*

CELIA: Would you like to take off your coat?

PIERRE: Thank you.

He removes his coat and hands it to her. She hangs it up by the door.

CELIA: I hope you drink coffee.

PIERRE: Yes.

She moves through to fetch the coffee tray.

PIERRE: It's generous of you to see me.

CELIA: It's what I do.

PIERRE is gazing around surreptitiously. He sees CELIA's row of notebooks on the shelf.

PIERRE: What's the name of this yellow flower, *la jonquille – en anglais* [the daffodil – in English]?

CELIA: Daffodils.

He smells them, but they have no smell.

PIERRE: Daffodils –

CELIA enters with the tray – on which is a cloth, two small, glazed mugs, a bowl of sugar and the coffee. Each object is beautiful, selected with care. She sets the tray down.

CELIA: Please make yourself at home.

PIERRE: At home?

CELIA: Take a seat.

PIERRE: Make myself at home. This is a way of saying please sit?

CELIA: It's a way of saying please relax.

He sits in an armchair at a right angle to the couch.

CELIA: So you're Pierre. You were very insistent on the phone.

PIERRE: Yes.

CELIA: Celia.

She offers her hand. He takes it and holds it.

PIERRE: I know.

CELIA: Pleased to meet you in the flesh.

PIERRE: Pleased to meet you. In the flesh.

CELIA: You look familiar. Haven't I seen you somewhere before?

PIERRE: I don't – perhaps.

She withdraws her hand, flushing slightly.

PIERRE: I have the money.

He tries to give her a few notes.

CELIA: Not now.

PIERRE: I must pay you every time, yes?

CELIA: I prefer it that way.

PIERRE: At the end?

CELIA: Yes.

PIERRE pockets his money.

PIERRE: You think once a week is enough?

CELIA: It's what we agreed to, isn't it?

PIERRE: Every Wednesday morning. Ten o'clock. For one hour and a half.

CELIA: Can you afford that?

PIERRE: Why not? You think I look too – what?

CELIA: I didn't mean anything by it.

PIERRE: I saved up.

CELIA: Well, let's see how we get along. If you're quick, perhaps we can meet a couple of times a week. For shorter periods.

PIERRE: I will like it.

CELIA: Would, not will. We're still being hypothetical.

Silence.

PIERRE: These books. They are impressive.

CELIA: Books are not in themselves impressive.

PIERRE: I mean you. To read these.

Silence.

PIERRE: And you always work from home?

CELIA: I try to. Although I've been cutting down on my working hours.

PIERRE: You said this in the phone.

CELIA: I'd decided not to take on anyone new. But you wouldn't take no for an answer.

PIERRE: No.

CELIA: There are several other places in Paris you could have gone. Why me?

PIERRE: You were recommended by one of the other students at the Sorbonne.

CELIA: I suppose you saw one of my notices. I didn't know they were still up.

PIERRE: They aren't.

Silence.

PIERRE: I kept your number with me. As I'm saying – I had to save up.

CELIA: I was a student there too. For a bit.

PIERRE: Why have you left?

CELIA: It's the past simple, not the past perfect.

PIERRE: Why did you leave?

CELIA: I was doing *le cours de lange et civilisation* [the course in language and civilisation]. The course ended.

Silence.

CELIA: Actually, I dropped out. I didn't feel comfortable
– trying to be a student again. I'd rather read the books by
myself. Form my own opinions.

PIERRE: I know what you mean.

Silence.

PIERRE: You live alone?

CELIA: You ask a lot of questions, Pierre.

PIERRE: Sorry.

CELIA: Shall I pour?

PIERRE: What is 'pour'?

CELIA: Pour the coffee.

PIERRE: Pour the coffee. Yes.

She pours the coffee. PIERRE is watching her every move.

CELIA: There we go.

She passes his coffee. He doesn't take sugar.

PIERRE: Thank you.

She glances at her watch.

CELIA: I suppose we'd better get on with it. You seem fairly
proficient.

PIERRE: I do?

CELIA: Have you taken English courses before?

PIERRE: In Dijon. At 'Language Works'. After I finished
school.

CELIA: So you know the terminology. The passive, the
different tenses and conditionals. Modal verbs and
subjunctives. And so on?

PIERRE: Some I maybe had forgotten.

CELIA: We'll need to revise your perfect tenses.

PIERRE: You will see that I learn quickly.

CELIA: Oh, I will, will I?

They regard each other intently – with a strange familiarity.

CELIA: So, Pierre. What are you hoping to get out of this?

PIERRE: I wanted you –

CELIA: Yes?

PIERRE: I thought: you will be the person to help me.

CELIA: Would. With what?

PIERRE: Everything. You would help me to – fit.

CELIA: Into what?

PIERRE: What is there. Around. Ahead.

Silence.

CELIA: I think you overestimate me.

PIERRE: And I want to express.

CELIA: What?

PIERRE: Myself.

CELIA: The verb 'to express' is a transitive verb. It takes an object. You have to express some thing. And the thing you cannot express is yourself?

PIERRE: I can't reveal myself. Through the words. The English words.

CELIA: Do you think any of us can do that?

PIERRE: Some better than the others.

CELIA: Words are better at misleading than revealing, in my experience. But you say you want to express yourself. To something. You have to have an object in mind. What is your object? To whom would you like to express yourself?

PIERRE: You are my object.

CELIA: For now, perhaps.

PIERRE: It's why I came.

CELIA: To be able to express yourself to an English person? In English?

PIERRE: If you like.

CELIA: Why English?

PIERRE: You mean – why not an African language? Swahili, or something like this?

CELIA: Something like 'that'. Swahili isn't here – it's out there, far away somewhere.

PIERRE: English is the language of the world. If you can speak it, you can live or work anywhere. Swahili? You know there's no point of 'that'.

CELIA: How are your listening skills?

PIERRE: I can read and listen. The speaking and the writing are more difficult.

CELIA: Those are the more generative skills. Listening and reading are more passive.

PIERRE: Yes.

CELIA: Perhaps we should consider the passive itself. It's a good test of a person's proficiency. You remember the basic model for the passive?

PIERRE: We use the past participle, I think.

CELIA: It's the verb 'to be' in whatever tense is necessary, plus the past participle.

PIERRE: The verb to be plus the past participle.

CELIA: Could you give me an example?

PIERRE: I was born?

CELIA: Yes. Because you can't give birth to yourself, can you? You rely on someone else for that. Another?

PIERRE: I am taught by you.

CELIA: That's right. Although you're 'being' taught by me, aren't you? It's happening now. The present continuous passive.

PIERRE: The passive in the present continuous.

CELIA: Let's start with something about yourself. What are you doing at the moment?

Silence.

PIERRE: I study the History of the Art.

CELIA: Present continuous. I am studying History of Art.

PIERRE: I am studying History of Art at the Sorbonne. And Western Philosophy. I do a course in Aristotle. Epicurius. Montaigne. Spinoza. John Stuart Mill.

CELIA: Has John Stuart Mill helped?

PIERRE: We haven't arrived at him yet.

CELIA: Reached. Do you paint?

PIERRE: I copy illustrations – *a l'aquarelle* [with watercolours]?

CELIA: With watercolours.

PIERRE: It's something I arrive to do when I am feeling – *pensif* [thoughtful/ sad].

CELIA: You needn't arrive. Although I know the French have to, even when they're already there. Perhaps it's why they're almost always late. The being there is not so important.

PIERRE: Was I late?

CELIA: No, Pierre. I was joking. An English joke. About the French.

PIERRE: Ah.

Silence.

CELIA: Humour has never been my strong point.

Silence.

CELIA: Although you were late. By about six minutes.

PIERRE: I was here for half an hour. Before. Waiting.

CELIA: And yet you were still six minutes late?

PIERRE: I went around the bend. For a walk. Then I came back.

Silence.

CELIA: Right. So – copying copies of other things. This is something you 'arrive to do' when you're feeling *pensif*?

PIERRE: Yes.

CELIA: Are you often sad?

PIERRE: No.

CELIA: Is that why you're not a 'proper' artist? Too much happiness?

PIERRE: No one is filled with too much happiness. But some unhappiness. It is normal, no?

CELIA: A degree of unhappiness is probably normal. I wouldn't know. Where did you grow up? Paris?

PIERRE: No.

CELIA: Well, where did you go to school?

PIERRE: In a village near Beaune. I went to school at a place named Seurre.

CELIA: You grew up in Seurre?

PIERRE: No.

CELIA: Are you finding this too boring to speak about? Would you rather talk about something else?

PIERRE: No.

CELIA: No?

PIERRE: No.

CELIA: Come on, Pierre. Express something. Surprise me. You aren't here to say 'no' to everything.

PIERRE: It's – difficult.

CELIA: It's what people expect. We have to learn to make up stories about ourselves. To represent ourselves.

PIERRE: Why?

CELIA: I suppose people want to see if your story fits into theirs.

PIERRE: You want me to make up the story?

CELIA: If you like. The actual facts are not always that important. It's how we present the facts that matters more. It's not important that my story is half fantasy. Something I want to be rather than what I am. My imagined parts, you see – they tell you something else. Something that might signify more. My desire. What I want. What I want to move towards. A sense of a future. We want to know that we share a similar sense of a future. The past can become – less significant. Are you following all this?

PIERRE: *(Lying.)* Yes.

Silence.

PIERRE: I have not thought about how to explain myself. In a story. Even in French.

CELIA: Let's begin at a beginning then. Tell me where you grew up.

PIERRE: In a small village next to Seurre. Pouilly-sur-Saone. Our house is on the *bord* [embankment] of the River Saone. This is where I have most of my childhood.

CELIA: Remember – it's far away. And you've already had your childhood.

PIERRE: That was where I had my childhood.

CELIA: Good. Although we usually spend our childhood. Like money. Something precious that's used up. Carry on.

PIERRE: About Pouilly? There's little to tell. It's a small place. Typical of the Bourgogne. One *boulangerie* [bakery], owned by a woman who hates all people and never smiles. Her husband runs the *tabac* [tobacconist].

CELIA: Tobacconist.

PIERRE: The husband also hates, but only his wife. Then there's the post office, with the diamond patterns on the roof. By the church, there's the monument for all the men who died in the war. The wars.

CELIA: Was it dull?

PIERRE: Not dull. It's very colourful in the summer. Of course, there's the River Saone.

CELIA: Tell me about the river.

PIERRE: It's wide, yes? My bedroom sits in the roof of the house. *Dans la mansarde* [in the attic].

CELIA: Attic.

PIERRE: When I open my window, I see the *tilleul* [lime] trees. Huge and soft. The river all below me. When I was younger, I had this yellow kayak that I liked to paddle. In the summer the river is warm, so you can swim.

CELIA: And in the winter?

PIERRE: The water grows high. It 'pours' out on the other side. From my bedroom window, it's like I am living on the side of a long lake, without an end, floating.

CELIA: A country boy. Altogether *provençal* [of the provinces]. Do you have brothers, sisters?

PIERRE: There's only me.

CELIA: So what was it like – arriving in Paris?

PIERRE: Fine.

CELIA: Don't you miss your home?

PIERRE: Sometimes. This is when I'm feeling sad.

CELIA: Are you feeling sad now?

PIERRE: No.

CELIA: Then use the present simple.

PIERRE: Sorry.

CELIA: But when you're feeling sad, you copy things. What do you copy?

PIERRE: I copy pictures of the birds. The birds of Pouilly.

CELIA: Tell me about the birds.

PIERRE: I like to watch them during the day. *Les martin-pecheurs.* The little blue fishing birds.

CELIA: Kingfishers.

PIERRE: *Et les rossignols* in the evenings. These are the nightingales. These I know the name for. Sometimes there are five or ten or fifteen of the nightingales singing in the same time. When it's spring, like now, they are singing all in the one time. I imitate them. I make the sound of many birds. Sometimes, they will answer me.

CELIA: They all sing. A general rule. Present simple. What else?

PIERRE: *Les guêpiers.*

CELIA: Wasps?

PIERRE: Bees. Bee-eaters, I think.

Celia shrugs.

PIERRE: These birds are bright as jewels. They are all the way from Africa during the summer. They nest in the river cliffs.

CELIA: All the way from Africa?

PIERRE: Yes.

Silence.

CELIA: It sounds a bit too perfect, Pierre. Is that all there is to you? A kayak and some nightingales?

PIERRE: What do you desire me to say?

CELIA: I want you to express yourself. Risk something. Tell me a story you're a bit embarrassed about. We only learn to speak fully in a language when we've found something – electric to express. You can say anything. As I say, it doesn't even have to be literally true.

Silence.

CELIA: Would you like more coffee?

PIERRE: No, thank you.

Silence.

CELIA: Surely you have a girl you care about?

PIERRE: No.

Silence.

PIERRE: Yes.

CELIA: Which?

PIERRE: Yes.

CELIA: A girlfriend?

PIERRE: I do not have a girlfriend at the moment.

CELIA: Really?

PIERRE: I have a girlfriend during two years. Back in Pouilly. Elodie. No girlfriend now.

CELIA: For two years? What you mean is that you had a girlfriend. Elodie. For two years. It was a fixed period of time. But now it's finished. Yes?

PIERRE: It's finished. I have a girlfriend for two years.

CELIA: Had a girlfriend. You had her. But the relationship is over. It's gone.

PIERRE: Yes – gone.

Silence.

PIERRE: I never loved her.

CELIA: I think you did. Otherwise you wouldn't say it like that.

PIERRE: Now I love someone else.

CELIA: Oh. And who's that?

PIERRE: She doesn't know.

CELIA: Is she seeing someone else?

PIERRE: I think she's alone.

CELIA: Perhaps you should tell her.

PIERRE: I don't know how to express it.

CELIA: Of course you do. You simply say the words 'I love you'. The words will go as far as words can go in expressing it. Whatever 'it' is.

PIERRE: She doesn't know me so well.

CELIA: In time, she can get to know you better.

PIERRE: She has only seen me the once.

CELIA: Then you must try to see her 'the twice'.

PIERRE: I will.

Silence.

CELIA: But how can you know?

PIERRE: Know?

CELIA: How can you be in love with her when you've only seen her once?

PIERRE: I've seen her many times. It's that she doesn't see me.

CELIA: What do you mean?

PIERRE: She lives in the same street as I do. La rue St-Jacques. At the other side of the city. I see her in the supermarket, choosing the cheese. At the bookshop, buying the books. I've even walked behind her in the *Jardin du Luxembourg* [Luxembourg Gardens].

CELIA: I see.

PIERRE: I've discovered many things about her.

CELIA: Like what cheese she chooses?

PIERRE: Yes.

CELIA: You follow her about?

PIERRE: No, no – or not for long.

CELIA regards him.

CELIA: How do you know that you even like this woman? It's clearly more about you than her. Alright, you know she buys Comté instead of Emmenthal –

PIERRE: Manchego, actually – the sheep's milk cheese from Spain.

CELIA: Right. But I'm sure many people buy that.

PIERRE: I also see the way she smiles. She can hold her head to the one side – as if she's listening to something I can't hear.

CELIA: She's just anyone.

PIERRE: No, she isn't.

CELIA: She's probably a nutcase.

PIERRE: She's the one I was waiting for.

CELIA: Have been waiting for. It continues into the present, doesn't it?

PIERRE: Yes.

Silence.

CELIA: My advice is that you leave her alone. When you project your desires onto other people, you can only disappoint yourself.

Silence.

PIERRE: The coffee. Please. I will have it now. I change my mind.

CELIA: Have changed it. You changed your mind, but we don't know exactly when.

She takes the coffee through to the kitchen area and switches on the kettle.

PIERRE: You're right. There is more to me than – the nightingales.

During the following, PIERRE stands – he goes over to the bookshelves where CELIA keeps her notebooks in a row. CELIA is occupied in the kitchen area.

CELIA: Oh yes?

PIERRE: I want to tell you everything.

CELIA: Well, it needn't be everything.

PIERRE: I know you are wanting to help.

CELIA: I want to help. A general fact. Not something I am only doing in the present. As a temporary activity.

PIERRE: The present simple – yes.

PIERRE takes out one of the notebooks. He hears CELIA coming and doesn't have time to put it back. He hides it behind his back.

CELIA enters. PIERRE stuffs the notebook into his trousers behind his back.

CELIA: What was it?

PIERRE: What?

CELIA: What did you want to say?

Silence.

PIERRE: I am from Africa.

CELIA: Like those – wasp birds?

PIERRE: *Oui, comme les guêpiers* [Yes, like the bee-eaters]?

CELIA: Did something bad happen to you. There in Africa?

PIERRE: Something bad happens to many people – there in Africa.

CELIA: Well, I wouldn't be put off. I'm a good listener. My brother used to call me his agony aunt. He said I take a deep delight in the dark side. It was a joke, of course. Another English joke.

PIERRE: Of course.

CELIA: My mother has spent a lot of time in Africa. She's a journalist. You know the *Guardian* newspaper?

PIERRE: *(Lying.)* Yes.

CELIA: She went all over the continent. Ethiopia, Zimbabwe, Rwanda. She loved it there. Where's your family from originally? Is it somewhere – conflicted?

PIERRE: Something like that.

CELIA: Good. I mean, it's good that you said 'that' and not 'this'. I didn't mean –

Silence.

PIERRE: I think I need time to – think. About my story. In English. Can I prepare it for another time?

CELIA: If you like. It might be better to call it a day. I mean for today.

PIERRE: Please – no.

CELIA: I needn't charge you. This can be an introductory session. A getting to know each other. Before the actual start.

PIERRE: I want to continue with this lesson. Not call it a day. I must continue with practicing the passive.

The kettle is boiling in the kitchen.

Blackout.

Part Two

NARRATIVE TENSES

CELIA's apartment. There is thunder outside. Rain. CELIA is pouring fresh water into the daffodils when the phone rings.

She picks up the phone.

CELIA: *Allô?* [Hello]?

Silence.

CELIA: Oh hello, Mum.

Silence.

CELIA: He does?

Silence.

CELIA: Can't he pick up the phone and tell me himself?

Silence.

CELIA: So what's the big news?

Silence.

CELIA: He's getting – ? No!

Silence.

CELIA: To whom?

Silence.

CELIA: I see.

Silence.

CELIA: I can't talk about this right now, Mum. I have a student waiting in the sitting-room.

Silence.

CELIA: A boy.

Silence.

CELIA: He's extremely attractive.

Silence.

CELIA: Oh Mum – really. Bye.

She hangs up. On the table are a banana, a knife and a plate. She sits and cuts the banana in half. She starts to eat one of the halves. She stares ahead for a long time. Tears are streaming down her face.

The doorbell rings. She wipes her eyes and goes to answer the door.

PIERRE enters. There is no evidence that CELIA has been upset.

PIERRE: Hello.

CELIA: Is it still raining outside?

PIERRE: It is.

CELIA: Your hair is sparkling.

PIERRE: Sparkling?

CELIA: Glittering. Like there are little stars inside it.

PIERRE: There are stars inside my hair?

CELIA: Yes.

Silence.

CELIA: Come in.

PIERRE: I will make myself at home.

CELIA: You have to be invited to do that.

PIERRE: Invited to relax?

CELIA: I suppose the expression means that you can behave as you do at home. Not stand on formality.

PIERRE: How 'stand on' formality?

CELIA: It means that you can sit, I suppose – put your feet up. Though not literally, of course.

PIERRE is thoroughly confused.

PIERRE: *Les anglais!* [The English!]

CELIA goes through to the kitchen area to fetch the coffee tray – the coffee has been made already. There are two ginger biscuits on a plate – and the same small mugs.

PIERRE has CELIA's notebook. He's about to take it out to return it to the shelves when Celia enters.

CELIA: Black. No sugar.

PIERRE: You remember.

CELIA: Absolutely everything.

They sit and take a moment to watch the rain outside. Then CELIA pours his coffee. Her hands are shaking slightly. She spills the coffee.

CELIA: Damn.

She takes the cloth from the tray and cleans up the coffee.

CELIA: I don't know what's got into me today.

PIERRE: You have cold?

CELIA: You say 'Are you cold?' when you want to know if someone's cold, and 'Do you have a cold?' if you think someone's ill.

PIERRE: Are you cold?

CELIA: No.

PIERRE: Do you have cold?

CELIA: A cold. No.

PIERRE: Then why do you shake your hands?

CELIA: I don't shake them. They are simply shaking themselves. Perhaps it's my blood sugar. I have problems with that. But we use the present continuous. Because they are shaking now. If I say my hands shake, we are using the present simple and talking about a general habit or situation. And my hands, they don't shake all the time. They don't shake generally.

PIERRE: The present continuous. I remember that.

CELIA: You *will* remember it. In the future. Future simple.

She passes him the coffee.

PIERRE: You do this every time? With every student?

CELIA: Sorry?

PIERRE: Drink coffee. Eat the biscuits.

CELIA: Sometimes. If people live across the river, I can agree to meet them half way. At a cafe. I usually take the bus to the Louvre. I have one student I meet near the Musée Rodin. He's rather ancient. Italian. Monsieur Levi. He once said something – odd. I can only be happy as long as I do not know myself.

Silence.

CELIA: Ignorance is bliss. You know the expression?

PIERRE: *(Lying.)* Yes.

CELIA: You have been to the Musée, of course?

PIERRE: No, never.

CELIA: No wonder you're not a proper artist! It's one of my favourite places in Paris. The house where Rodin lived, the gardens running all around it. It's the small marble works I love the most. They look as though they're made of wax. They glow. I suppose they absorb the light around them somehow. Is that how it works?

PIERRE: I don't know.

CELIA: 'The Centuaress' – the body of the woman melding into the body of a beast.

Silence.

CELIA: You can buy a season ticket for the gardens. We could have the lessons there if you liked.

PIERRE: I prefer it here.

He sips the coffee.

CELIA: Is it how you like it?

PIERRE: It is perfect.

CELIA: Ginger biscuit?

PIERRE: Thanks.

He takes a biscuit.

CELIA: *(Rather proud.)* That's my breakfast.

PIERRE: A biscuit is what you have for the breakfast?

CELIA: And half a banana. Yes.

They gaze at the other half of the banana still on the table.

CELIA: You can have it if you like.

PIERRE: Thanks.

He picks up the remaining half of the banana and eats it. She watches him closely.

CELIA: I never have anything else for breakfast.

Silence – PIERRE eating.

CELIA: So our grammar point for the day is narrative tenses.

He says nothing.

CELIA: Past simple, past continuous, past perfect. You know these terms?

PIERRE: I know.

CELIA: I'd like you to describe a day using the past tenses. It can be any kind of day. A happy day, a sad day, a boring day, a perfect day. But remember: we mainly narrate stories in the past simple.

PIERRE considers.

PIERRE: I describe a happy day.

CELIA: Will describe. Future simple. Okay.

PIERRE: When I wake. Sorry. Woke.

CELIA: Up. You woke up. A modal verb in the past simple. Yes?

PIERRE: When I woke up, I stretched myself with my arms wide and – got out of my bed.

CELIA: Had you slept well? It's an event even further back in time from the series of events being described, so it takes the past perfect tense.

PIERRE: I had slept well.

CELIA: Good.

PIERRE: I had dreamed a dream.

CELIA: You had dreamt it. What was it about?

Silence.

PIERRE: A girl. I had dreamt a beautiful girl.

CELIA: I see. Go on. You got out of bed?

PIERRE: I got out of bed. I went to the shower. I turned it on and stood under the water and I washed me.

CELIA: Myself.

PIERRE: Myself. Then I finished and I dried 'myself' with the towel.

CELIA: What colour is your towel?

PIERRE: It is a blue towel.

CELIA: What kind of blue?

PIERRE: Dark blue.

CELIA: What kind of dark blue?

PIERRE: Like the night.

CELIA: Go on.

PIERRE: Then I go to my bedroom and open my cupboard.

CELIA: So you opened your cupboard.

PIERRE: I opened my cupboard and took my clothes.

CELIA: Describe your clothes.

PIERRE: I took a green T-shirt. And a jean. A pair of jean.

CELIA: Jeans.

PIERRE: And my pullover, what is dark blue. Also like the night. And my socks.

Silence.

CELIA: The clothes you're wearing now. Your happy day is today?

PIERRE: Yes.

CELIA: Go on. What else?

PIERRE: Also I took my – what must I say for it?

CELIA: What?

PIERRE: *Mon slip.* My boxing shorts.

CELIA: Boxer shorts. Underpants.

PIERRE: Underpants.

CELIA: And what colour are those?

PIERRE: Blue. Those are blue.

CELIA: Like the night?

PIERRE: Like the day.

Silence.

CELIA: And what did you do then?

PIERRE: I dressed me – myself – and I left my room.

CELIA: Was the sun shining?

PIERRE: No. The rain was raining. It was raining. My hair got wet. My hair was – sprinkling?

CELIA: Sparkling.

PIERRE: Sparkling.

CELIA: And then?

He looks at her directly.

PIERRE: Then I went to the Metro. I catch the train to Lamarck Caulaincourt. Caught. I caught it. I get out the train and I take the lift up. Then I enter the light and go down the stairs, past that café where I like to go – Le Refuge.

CELIA: I like to go there too!

PIERRE: You do? And so I come here.

CELIA: Yes, you came. And it was still raining.

PIERRE: It was still raining. And when you arrived at the door and saw me, you said to me that I have stars inside my hair.

CELIA: I did. You do. And then what happened?

PIERRE: I am not sure.

The phone buzzes. They do not move. CELIA glares at it.

PIERRE: I do not mind. Please take it.

She picks up the phone and answers.

CELIA: *Allô?*

She goes through to the bedroom.

CELIA: *Monsieur Levi? Je vais venir cet après-midi. Est-ce que ça va?* [Hello. Mr Levi? I will come this afternoon. Is that okay?]

PIERRE takes out the notebook he took during the previous lesson. He goes over to the bookshelves to replace the notebook – and is still doing so when CELIA re-enters and sees him.

CELIA: *(Still on the phone.) Merci, monsieur. Au revoir.* [Thanks. Goodbye.] What are you doing, Pierre?

PIERRE: I was looking at a book.

CELIA: Why?

PIERRE: I thought it was a workbook. With lessons inside.

CELIA: I don't believe that. You were prying through my private things.

PIERRE: What is prying?

CELIA: You know exactly what it means. What do you want?

PIERRE: What?

CELIA: What have you come here for?

PIERRE: English lessons.

CELIA: There's some other thing going on here that I'm not even aware about, isn't there?

PIERRE: Maybe. It's nothing – bad.

CELIA: I have no idea who you are.

Silence.

PIERRE: Listen, I'm sorry I go through your stuff – went. I don't mean to be prying.

CELIA: It's something you did by mistake, is that it?

PIERRE: No, I was – uneasy.

CELIA: Well, you're not the only one. The way you come in here and look at everything. The way you look at me. Not as a student. Not as you should – were you polite. It makes me profoundly uneasy.

PIERRE: Why, because I'm black?

CELIA: What? That's absolutely not what I'm talking about.

PIERRE: Isn't it? I think it's the exact thing we're talking about. Can I afford to pay? Why aren't I learning Swahali?

CELIA: I never even said that! You said that!

PIERRE: I'm the one from the heart of darkness, yes?

CELIA: Pierre, for God's sake!

PIERRE: Don't worry. I've read that book. The cannibals that come out of the bush. The forest of heads on the sticks, all along the river. Open your books to page number twenty six! And me – the only dark one there!

CELIA: I don't know what you're going on about. This has nothing to do with race – it's about mutual respect!

PIERRE: Exactly! You pretend you want to help. You act all nice. But deep down you are always thinking – thank God I'm not like him. Always needing help. Thank God I'm civilised!

CELIA: This is – mad!

PIERRE: I know it's mad!

CELIA: You're turning me into something I'm not.

PIERRE: And you aren't doing the same to me?

CELIA: Well, what are you then?

PIERRE: I wish I knew!

Silence.

PIERRE: Whenever I close my eyes and stop, I see them. Even in the streets of Paris, or coming out the Metro. Always, I am carrying them in my head.

CELIA: Who?

PIERRE: They come when we are still asleep. Before the sun is come up.

CELIA: Is this some sort of – dream?

PIERRE: When they look at you, they don't see you. They have too many ants inside their head.

CELIA: But who are they?

PIERRE: Boys mostly. All of them – blind.

CELIA: I need you to explain yourself.

PIERRE: I know you do.

CELIA: I want to understand!

PIERRE: They are the Interhamwe.

CELIA: The who?

PIERRE: You don't even know who they are!

CELIA: No. Are they phantoms? Spirits? What?

PIERRE: They are like the walking dead – yes. But they carry guns. Children with guns who kill hundreds every week. The Interhamwe are the Hutu militias that are coming from Rwanda.

CELIA: You are saying you're from – Rwanda?

PIERRE: No, the Congo. They ask for money. If you give, they kill you. If you don't, they kill you. My father's genitals they cut out and throw them in the yard. My mother and my sisters they rape.

CELIA: I can't –

PIERRE: Because the sun is not come up, I slip away. Into the bush. Across the old banana plantation.

Silence.

PIERRE: I ran away. I fled. I left them there to die!

CELIA says nothing.

PIERRE: Is that enough darkness for you?

PIERRE is almost weeping with rage and remorse.

PIERRE: Are you satisfied?

Silence.

PIERRE: All the people were killed. Even the dogs. Thrown on a mountain of bodies to be burned.

CELIA: My God.

PIERRE: I was taken by the *medicins sans frontiers* [doctors without borders]. I was brought to France. Given to a white family in the Bourgogne. To be adopted. And that – is it. That is how I came to be at Pouilly.

Silence.

CELIA: Why are you telling me all this now?

PIERRE: It's what you want to hear, isn't it?

CELIA: No.

Silence.

CELIA: Yes.

Silence.

PIERRE: When you look at me, it's what you expect.

CELIA's phone starts buzzing. They don't move.

CELIA: I don't know what to expect.

Silence.

PIERRE: Who is this – Oliver?

CELIA: What?

PIERRE: I saw his name. In your book.

CELIA: He's my brother.

PIERRE: He's older than you?

CELIA: Twenty minutes younger.

PIERRE: And where is he now?

CELIA: I really can't talk about it.

The phone is still buzzing.

Blackout.

Part Three

THE CONDITIONAL

CELIA's apartment. Darkness. The phone is still buzzing. It stops.

Light grows. CELIA is on the couch, posing, while PIERRE sketches her.

The phone beeps.

CELIA: Today we are learning about articulating conditions. If you do this, I do that. They're called conditionals.

Pierre glances at her phone.

PIERRE: Why do you never answer your phone?

CELIA: Have you done your homework?

PIERRE: It's the way you look at it.

CELIA: Have you prepared something?

PIERRE: You think it will bite you?

CELIA: We should probably start with the zero conditional.

PIERRE: Or is there a person who wants to bite?

CELIA: What's the model for the zero conditional?

PIERRE: Present tense plus present tense?

CELIA: Give me an example.

PIERRE: You never say about yourself. You make me say about myself. But you are always asking the questions.

CELIA: I ask the questions because I am teaching you how to speak English. I already know how to speak it.

PIERRE: So when you can speak English, there's no longer a need to talk?

CELIA: My job is to pass on what I know until you can speak for yourself. It's not to tell you about myself.

PIERRE: Then change your job.

CELIA: You should've been content with what you had before you came here.

PIERRE: I want what you have.

CELIA: Oh, and what's that?

PIERRE: The world.

CELIA laughs.

PIERRE: You're beautiful, clever, rich. Most of all, you're white. You can go anywhere, always a bit higher than everything else.

CELIA: That's not a very nice thing to say.

PIERRE: Maybe you don't see it because for you it's normal. Or you do see it, but you don't like it to be said. You don't know what it is to be made always a bit lower than everything. Always – suspicious.

CELIA: The only person who can free you from that feeling is you. There are bigots everywhere – and they'll always pick on something, whoever you are.

PIERRE: You could try to help. By letting me in. By telling about yourself. As an equal. A friend.

CELIA: We're student and teacher. You came here so I could correct your grammar.

PIERRE: That's not why I came.

CELIA: Okay – you wanted to express yourself. Aren't you doing that? Aren't you getting from me exactly what you wanted?

PIERRE: Not exactly.

CELIA: Then what do you want – exactly?

PIERRE: I'll tell you when you're – softer.

CELIA: Listen, I've never been softer in my life.

Silence.

CELIA: Present tense plus present tense. Try to think of an example.

PIERRE: *(Still trying to draw her.)* Keep still. You keep moving your head.

CELIA: Can't you give it a break?

PIERRE: I'm accustomed to drawing birds – not English girls.

CELIA: The zero conditional.

PIERRE: If he gives himself, she will give herself?

CELIA: Is that what you prepared for me? Anyway – you're wrong. You've slipped into the future simple. It should be: if he gives, she gives. But the zero conditional is not very common. Such clear causality is rare.

PIERRE: You're – losing me.

CELIA: The zero conditional is used for things like scientific experiments. Not everyday life. If you heat water to a hundred degrees, it boils. Humans need a greater deal of uncertainty to express themselves. They don't obey the laws of Science.

PIERRE: *(Still drawing.)* Stop moving!

CELIA: I want to see for myself.

She comes over to look at the drawing. He hides it.

PIERRE: Not yet!

She sits.

PIERRE: Look towards the sky.

CELIA: It's called the ceiling.

He continues drawing.

CELIA: What about the model for the first conditional?

PIERRE: Present simple plus future simple? If he likes her, she will like him?

CELIA: Correct, but slightly presumptuous. It could be: if he likes her, she will consider him.

He continues drawing her for a while.

PIERRE: Why do you not want to talk about yourself?

CELIA: Can't you accept that I am what you see? Isn't that enough?

PIERRE: You said we must make up stories to represent ourselves.

CELIA: Well then I'll make it up in the present. With you. As we go along. Why should stories from the past – whether hideous or dull – represent us? Can't we free ourselves from what happened? Or do we always have to drag it along behind us – like some sort of hideous afterbirth? You didn't choose what happened to you. And neither did I.

PIERRE: What happened to you?

CELIA: Nothing.

PIERRE: Then what did you do?

Silence.

PIERRE: Or not do?

Silence.

CELIA: Tell me the model for the second conditional.

PIERRE: Past simple plus – present simple? I can't remember.

She gets up – pretending to walk towards the kitchen.

PIERRE: What are you doing?

She snatches the pad from him.

CELIA: And who is that supposed to be!

PIERRE: Don't you like it?

CELIA: It looks like an illustration from a magazine.

PIERRE picks up her phone.

PIERRE: You have seven missed calls.

CELIA: Give that back!

PIERRE holds out the phone – and they swap the phone and the pad.

CELIA: My mother is the only person who phones me these days. For your information. And Monsieur Levi.

PIERRE: How do I know this Monsieur Levi isn't your lover?

CELIA: He's as blind as a bat.

PIERRE: He doesn't need eyes in order to kiss you.

CELIA: Well, I would have to tear mine out in order to kiss him.

PIERRE: And you have no other students?

CELIA: I told you: my only other student at the moment is you.

PIERRE tears up his sketch of CELIA.

CELIA: Why did you do that?

PIERRE: I must start again.

CELIA: That is such a violent thing to do to me.

PIERRE: You said it wasn't you.

CELIA: Well, it's as close as you could get.

PIERRE: I want to make it look more alive.

CELIA: You mean me – you want me to look more alive.

He starts again.

CELIA: The second conditional is past simple plus future simple. If he wanted to draw her, she would let him.

PIERRE: If he wanted to draw her, she would let him?

CELIA: Yes.

He continues drawing.

CELIA: Don't look at the drawing. Look at me and let your hand move across the page.

He starts again.

CELIA: It's called contour drawing. You don't concern yourself with the page – you only look at the subject. It's supposed to help you to see directly, without interpretation.

He does this for a while.

CELIA: Let's see.

He hands her the drawing. She looks at it and laughs. He looks at it with her.

PIERRE: The eye looks a bit like yours, don't you think?

CELIA: *(Laughing.)* Which bit of this pile of spaghetti are you referring to exactly?

PIERRE: And the way the hair falls – there.

He touches her hair and pushes a strand of it back.

CELIA: You're very sweet, you know that?

PIERRE: If he wanted –

CELIA: What?

PIERRE: The second conditional. If he wanted to –

CELIA: Yes?

PIERRE: Touch her. She would let him?

Silence.

PIERRE: Is that correct?

Silence.

CELIA: Yes. No.

PIERRE: No?

Silence.

PIERRE: Yes?

CELIA: I meant that was the correct use of the second conditional.

PIERRE: Yes?

CELIA: No.

Silence.

CELIA: She would not let him touch her if he wanted to.

PIERRE says nothing.

CELIA: You see, you can swap the clauses around with conditionals. They still work.

Silence.

CELIA: I think we'd better stop – for today.

PIERRE: I am paying for one hour.

CELIA: I don't like being paid for this.

Silence.

PIERRE: You think I don't understand?

CELIA: What?

PIERRE: Everything.

CELIA: How can you – when I don't myself?

PIERRE: Everyone knows everything. But we hide from it.

CELIA: Your English is improving.

She is trembling slightly.

PIERRE: Why are you shaking?

CELIA: That's good. The present continuous.

PIERRE: *C'est pas le moment de me faire un cours d'anglais.* [This is not the moment for an English lesson.]

CELIA: It's exactly the moment for an English lesson.

PIERRE: I want to kiss you.

CELIA: The third conditional. We haven't done it yet. It requires the past perfect and the present perfect with the – the subjunctive. I forget.

PIERRE: If he had touched her, then she might – have wanted it?

CELIA: Yes – something along those lines.

PIERRE touches her face.

CELIA: I grew up in Primrose Hill. With my brother. And my mother. Did I tell you that?

PIERRE: Now you want to talk?

Her whole body is shuddering slightly.

CELIA: We lived in Chalcott Square.

PIERRE: It sounds pretty.

CELIA: We had a Japanese garden at the back. My brother and I had the job of collecting the snails. We would take them to the railway bridge in a bucket and let them go in the willowherb.

PIERRE: How lovely.

CELIA: Are you listening?

PIERRE: You throw the snails in the willowherb.

CELIA: My mother was often away.

PIERRE: Why away?

CELIA: For months at a time. In Africa somewhere. Writing her next book.

PIERRE: Ah yes.

CELIA: She was always a little in love with African men. She said she found them sexy. I think she had several affairs. But she always left them there – where she'd found them.

PIERRE: Very sensible.

CELIA: She'd come back from each trip with gifts for me and Oliver. Dolls made from beads. Carved wooden figures with straw coming out their heads.

PIERRE: *(Ironic.)* Black magic.

CELIA: She'd find you – alluring. And want to know everything about you. She'd probably put you in a book. You know her books have been translated into nine different languages? Perhaps you've read one of them. She's popular throughout Europe.

PIERRE: Are you nervous? Your whole body – it is shaking.

CELIA: My father was a surgeon. I was always a bit – dim. Around him.

PIERRE: Dim?

CELIA: Out of focus as well as stupid. Like we were not where he was. He left when we were about ten.

PIERRE takes her hand.

CELIA: Both my parents are considered a great success. Olly too. I've somehow become the family flop. Sitting here, teaching people like you. It's not what anyone imagined for me. I was supposed to be – exceptional. I was going to be an actress, then a novelist. I won't even manage being a mother at this rate. And as for teaching English –

PIERRE: Celia, I'm not here to learn English.

CELIA: We shouldn't even be doing this.

PIERRE: Because you're my teacher? I'm not a child.

CELIA: Please – don't.

She withdraws her hand.

PIERRE: Alright. I won't touch. But we can speak. Yes?

CELIA: Yes.

PIERRE: Tell me a thing you have never told to anyone. Something – dangerous. I want to know everything about you.

CELIA: People say that but they never really mean it.

PIERRE: I gave a secret part of me. Now I want one from you.

They stare at each other.

CELIA: Do you know how to keep your mouth shut?

PIERRE demonstrates how he can keep his mouth shut – and nods.

CELIA: Well, I suppose I could tell you that I take things. Is that enough?

PIERRE: What do you take?

CELIA: Sometimes things from shops.

PIERRE: What things from shops?

CELIA: Oh, silly things. Nail varnish. Lip balm. A nail file.

PIERRE: Why?

CELIA: I suppose I imagine I'm not worthy.

PIERRE: To buy it?

CELIA: Of buying it for myself. I've never bothered to understand it. But I take things. From shops and from places I stay. Mostly from relatives – and from friends. Usually things they wouldn't even miss. Like a comb, or soap. Sometimes I take a book.

PIERRE: When did it begin?

CELIA: Start. You say start. It started when I was about twelve, thirteen.

Silence.

CELIA: We could talk about it all day and not get to the bottom of it.

PIERRE: Which of these books did you take?

CELIA: That one there. Rilke's poems. I took that from my father's study.

PIERRE: After he left or before?

CELIA: After, of course.

PIERRE: But that's not stealing.

CELIA: I took *Sons and Lovers* from a friend who lives in Surrey. From her parents' house, in fact. I take books whenever I go there. Rebecca's parents is where I got most of my Virginia Woolf. Would you like me to carry on? For a while I worked at a bookshop. I stole a great many books from there. All my Everyman's Library. That entire row.

PIERRE: You must try to stop.

CELIA: I am.

PIERRE: Good.

Silence.

PIERRE: Why do you do it?

CELIA: I suppose I like the thrill. Living with the guilt. Having something I can focus on and feel particularly bad about. I mean bad in a particular sense – rather than just generally.

Silence.

CELIA: Now you – you tell me something.

PIERRE: My secret? But I already have.

CELIA: Another one then.

PIERRE: I – can't think of a small one.

CELIA: Only big ones?

PIERRE: *(Laughing.)* Yes!

Silence.

CELIA: Alright. A big one then.

PIERRE: I have one that is involved with you.

CELIA: Oh yes?

PIERRE: It's that I saw you first wearing a yellow dress.

CELIA: Which yellow dress?

PIERRE: The one that is simple – your arms bare *(demonstrating)* to here – going to the length of your knees.

CELIA: Ah that. Yes – I stole that dress from Le Bon Marché!

PIERRE: Well, you were wearing it when I saw you at the Sorbonne, putting up your notices. It was still September then. Autumn.

CELIA: Oh.

Silence.

CELIA: When you first came here, you said there was this girl. In the Luxembourg Gardens. The girl you were watching. Me?

PIERRE: I used to see you at the Sorbonne.

CELIA: I've never bought sheep's milk cheese from Spain in my life.

PIERRE: Well, I made that bit up.

CELIA: I don't even remember going food shopping around there. Why would I? There's a perfectly good place next door.

PIERRE: When I first saw you at the Sorbonne, I took down your number and your address. When you disappeared, I called – but there was no reply.

CELIA: There rarely is!

PIERRE: So I decided to come up here. To see where you live.

CELIA: The psychologists call it scopophilia. It's an illness. There's the pleasure of looking and the pleasure of being looked at. Objectifying others or objectifying yourself. It can become addictive if you're not careful. Would you describe yourself as a *voyeur*?

PIERRE: It was seeing you that made me into that.

CELIA: Right, so it's all my fault!

PIERRE: For being beautiful. Yes!

Silence.

CELIA: So you came up here to look at me. What happened next?

PIERRE: You left the apartment and went into the supermarket. I followed you in – and then I turned and left.

CELIA: And you only did this the once?

PIERRE: Maybe the twice.

CELIA: *(Rather pleased, in spite of herself.)* How absolutely hideous.

PIERRE: I know it wasn't right. I wanted to call again. But I had become too – nervous.

CELIA: Not as nervous as I would have been!

PIERRE: I thought: if I can get that English girl to like me, I can be alright.

Silence.

CELIA: Should I be calling the police?

PIERRE: I'm not dangerous.

Silence.

CELIA: When you were watching me. What did I do?

Even PIERRE can sense she's relenting.

PIERRE: Many things. Like brushing your hair by the window. It was longer then. Reading your books at Le Refuge. Walking to the Cimetière de Montmartre – to Truffaut's grave. Buying goat milk cheese and *tartelettes citron* [lemon tarts].

CELIA: I think I should definitely be calling the police!

PIERRE: I followed you up the hill to Montmartre once. You stopped outside Au Lapin Agile and took off your sandals. You went past the grape vines, up through the tourist shops. It was getting dark. Sacré Couer was lit up on the hill. Outside, there were people playing the drums, smoking hashish, kissing – but you went up the stairs and into the church, and sat near the front, staring at the huge Christ in the dome, with his arms spread wide. The altar was made of gold. There was a single nun standing in front of it. She lifted her arms and started to sing. Like an angel. It was as if you were about to step up into heaven. The nun, she lifted her arms again and all the people in the church started to sing.

CELIA: I remember how beautiful it was. It made one imagine there could be a God. I'm not sure I like the idea of you watching me right then.

PIERRE: I could see how alone you looked. Sitting there, so upright, with the drums playing outside. It's why I was finally courageous enough to phone. I thought with you I might have a chance.

CELIA: I should probably be booting you out.

PIERRE: Should you?

CELIA: Somehow, I'm not afraid of you at all. You're about as dotty as me!

PIERRE: You aren't 'dotty'.

CELIA: You have no idea.

Silence.

CELIA: I want to look at your feet.

PIERRE: What?

CELIA: My grandmother always said – you can judge a man by his hands and his feet. I've already seen your hands. Now I want to look at your feet.

PIERRE, amused, takes off his shoes and his socks.

CELIA: So you followed me, did you – with those feet?

PIERRE: With those feet. What do you think?

She touches them, feels his soles.

CELIA: I say 'those'. You say 'these'. Because they belong to you.

PIERRE: They can belong to you if you like.

CELIA: Granny always said: 'Never trust a man with soft hands and feet!'

PIERRE laughs.

PIERRE: In Pouilly my feet were firm, but I'm a Parisian now.

CELIA: A *flâneur* [one who walks around idly], with lovely long toes.

PIERRE: Now yours.

CELIA: My what?

PIERRE: My grandmother said – before you marry a girl, you must look at her feet.

CELIA: Marriage? Now let's not get too carried away!

She puts out her feet and allows him to remove her shoes for her.

CELIA: There. Those are my feet.

PIERRE: Can I touch them?

CELIA: If you like.

He touches her feet.

CELIA: You must have done this before.

PIERRE: Touched your feet?

CELIA: Been a bit of a stalker. Did you follow that other girlfriend about?

PIERRE: Elodie?

CELIA: The one you pretended not to love.

PIERRE: Yes.

CELIA: Tell me more about her.

PIERRE: But it's your turn to tell a bad thing.

CELIA: This time you go first.

PIERRE: Only if I can touch your feet.

CELIA: If I allow you to touch my feet, you will tell me. Which conditional is that?

PIERRE: The first!

CELIA: You're a clever boy.

Silence.

PIERRE: I am climbing a ladder and seeing a whole new world.

CELIA: Stick to the topic. You were telling me about Elodie.

PIERRE: Okay. It's late at night. And she's with Etienne. There's a streetlamp, lighting the tree they stand under. All around is darkness. And they kiss.

CELIA: And she was your girlfriend at the time – this Elodie?

PIERRE: Oh yes!

CELIA: Go on.

PIERRE: I only watch. I never confront. I follow them all the way back to where Elodie lives. They enter the house and go up to her room, which looks down on the street. I wait there until the light goes out.

CELIA: And were you friendly with this boy she was with?

PIERRE: Etienne was my closest friend!

Silence.

PIERRE: When I saw them together, something inside me broke.

CELIA: Poor Pierre. And you've had no other girlfriend since?

PIERRE: Only a prostitute once in Paris.

CELIA: I really don't want to know about that!

Silence.

PIERRE: I hate Paris.

CELIA: So do I.

PIERRE: It's supposed to be so romantic, but all I see is – dirt. When you have no money, you feel like dirt. But you don't know what I'm talking about. You're rich!

CELIA: Not exactly. But I suppose I can get by with odd jobs – odd jobs like you.

PIERRE: Thanks!

CELIA: There's a family trust. From my mother's side. I sometimes think it's the worst thing that ever happened to me.

PIERRE: That's because you're rich.

Silence.

PIERRE: Why did you come to live in Paris?

CELIA: To get away, I suppose.

PIERRE: From what?

CELIA: England. London. My family.

PIERRE: Why?

CELIA: I needed a fresh start.

PIERRE: Your mother. She's still going all the time to Africa?

CELIA: No – it's India now. The mysterious East!

PIERRE: And your brother?

CELIA: Oliver?

PIERRE: I thought you were close.

CELIA: A bit too close for comfort.

PIERRE: What is that?

CELIA: Do we need to go into it?

PIERRE: It's your turn to speak.

CELIA: Well, I had to get away from him because – he's sick.

PIERRE: Sick?

CELIA: He has – inappropriate thoughts. What the doctor calls intrusive thoughts.

PIERRE: Why intrusive?

CELIA: The idea is that the thoughts come from somewhere else. The outside. They're not his.

PIERRE: Who else's can they be?

CELIA: He wants to disown them. But they keep on intruding. They come when they're least wanted. For reasons of their own.

PIERRE: What does he think exactly?

CELIA: He thinks about doing things.

PIERRE: To who?

CELIA: To whom. He's the subject. I'm the object.

PIERRE: You're the object?

CELIA: Yes.

PIERRE: But what kind of things does he think about?

CELIA: For God's sake! You want me to spell it out?

PIERRE: Yes!

CELIA: He desires me. Alright? He wants to do things to me. At least – that's what the thoughts are. The intruding thoughts. He can't control them, but that's what they represent.

Silence.

CELIA: He's also a good boy. A good person. Not some freak.

PIERRE: Right.

CELIA: He's been destroyed by it. In ruins. It's not what he would have chosen for himself.

PIERRE: It? You mean you.

CELIA: It simply happened. There's nothing he or anyone else can do about it. But the more he worries about it, the more it happens.

PIERRE: I see.

CELIA: So I had to get away. For his own good – and mine. To give us all some peace.

Silence.

PIERRE: Why are you telling me this?

CELIA: Sometimes when I'm with you, it's as if I'm with him. I mean – you couldn't be more different. And I like you – in a totally separate way. But being with you makes me imagine I'm repeating something. Making the same – mistake.

PIERRE: I am not Oliver.

CELIA: And I am not Elodie.

Silence.

PIERRE: You think there can be a chance for us?

CELIA: Could.

PIERRE: Why do you look so afraid?

CELIA: I'm afraid of committing some – deep sin. I don't want to be like my mother.

PIERRE: Lying with a man who looks like one of your voodoo dolls?

CELIA: Just – lying.

PIERRE: Yes, with me.

CELIA: With you. To you. They're simply prepositions.

PIERRE: I love you.

CELIA: I don't know what that means.

PIERRE: I loved you from the moment I saw you at the Sorbonne.

The phone starts to ring.

CELIA: That'll be my mother. She'll want to know if I'm coming to the wedding.

PIERRE: The wedding?

CELIA: Oliver's wedding.

Silence.

CELIA: He doesn't love her. It's another ploy. To make me feel shit.

PIERRE: Don't answer it.

The phone is still buzzing.

CELIA: Thanks for tracking me down.

PIERRE: The girl in the yellow dress!

CELIA: Yes!

They laugh. PIERRE kisses her. She doesn't resist.

Fade to black

Part Four

LIES AND TRUTH

CELIA's apartment.

CELIA: So sometimes we say. Sometimes we speak. Sometimes we tell. Sometimes we talk. But these verbs are not interchangeable. What do we do with a lie and the truth?

PIERRE: I don't know what you want.

CELIA: Do we say a lie, speak a lie, tell a lie? Which?

PIERRE: I think we tell a lie.

CELIA: And the truth?

PIERRE: We tell the truth.

CELIA: Usually. We try to. And your mind?

PIERRE: You tell your mind.

CELIA: You speak your mind.

PIERRE: Speak your mind.

CELIA: And you talk nonsense and you say what you think. Got that?

PIERRE: You talk nonsense and you say what you think.

CELIA: Let's talk about lying first. There are a number of modal verbs and expressions we could consider. You can live a lie and tell a pack of lies. You can even lie through your teeth. Are you familiar with these?

PIERRE: I think so.

CELIA: To lie through your teeth isn't separable. The object can't come between the verb and the particle. But some modal verbs are always separable. You have to lie your way out of a situation. Here, the modal verb to 'lie out' is broken in half by the phrase 'your way'.

PIERRE: Is 'your way' the object?

CELIA: It's hard to explain. You simply have to learn modal verbs as units of meaning. Don't try to analyse their parts. Their parts are not always logical in themselves.

PIERRE: You're leaving me behind.

CELIA: For example, there's also the modal verb to 'make out'. You can make out with someone, which is to kiss them, or something – I don't exactly know as it's American. But the verb 'to make' and the particle 'out' do not have anything to do with kissing in themselves. 'Make' and 'out' have two entirely separate meanings from the expression to 'make out'. And the verb to 'make out' is inseparable in this case.

PIERRE: You're going too fast.

CELIA: 'Make out' can also become separable. But its meaning will change. You can say 'he will make an honest woman out of me'. Here, 'an honest woman' is the object, which comes in the middle of the modal verb – and the verb and particle 'make' and 'out' have entirely new meanings. As I say, you must learn these as units. In isolation. Don't try to analyse them. For logic. There is no logic. There's only learning it. Accepting it as something that already – exists.

Silence.

PIERRE: Are you alright?

CELIA: Absolutely. I'm fine. Sorry. I'll pause.

Silence.

PIERRE: Honesty is the best policy. That's another expression, no?

Silence.

PIERRE: Are we never going to talk about it?

CELIA: What's there to talk about? If there was something to talk about, surely you would have phoned? I waited all week. Silence. Then you arrive here today as if nothing's happcned.

PIERRE: Every Wednesday morning. Ten o'clock.

CELIA: What was it? You got what you wanted – and then I no longer mattered?

PIERRE: Of course you mattered.

CELIA: I thought we had a relationship.

PIERRE: We did.

CELIA: You said you loved me.

PIERRE: I did.

Silence.

CELIA: I do hope you're using your tenses deliberately.

Silence.

CELIA: Do you know how insane I went? All week, waiting for you to phone. Every time I went out, I even hoped you were following me again. I stopped at street corners so the imaginary you could catch up.

PIERRE: I don't know why you're blaming me for this.

CELIA: Sorry. Who else should I be blaming? The pope?

PIERRE: I thought you didn't want me.

CELIA: How could you possibly have thought that? I gave myself to you, didn't I? Completely!

PIERRE: It wasn't like that.

CELIA: But we made love! We lay over here – on the floor – and I let you do whatever you wanted. Was that nothing?

PIERRE: I thought it would be – everything.

CELIA: And then it wasn't. You thought I was something else. Something special. Floating a bit above everything. I never asked to be put on some pedestal.

PIERRE: Didn't you?

CELIA: You began despising me the moment I started to like you. You thought: her standards are too low; I can do better than this.

PIERRE: That isn't how it was.

CELIA: You think people are something to climb up. Like ladders! But when will it be enough? At what point will you be able to say – yes, here I am, this is me! I'm comfortable inside my own skin!

PIERRE: Please – stop it.

CELIA: But it's when we have a bit of power that we reveal ourselves, isn't it?

PIERRE: What did I reveal?

CELIA: That you're the same as the rest of the world –

PIERRE: And what's wrong with that?

CELIA: We never want what we've got. As soon as we see the drudgery of each other, we're put off. Oh, don't worry. I've felt that with every doomed relationship. I only thought you'd be different. Kinder. Genuinely interested. Wanting to see me properly – for all my failings.

PIERRE: I wanted to – reflect.

CELIA: What was there to 'reflect' on?

PIERRE: It all seemed so violent. Then afterwards, when you were sick, and told me to get out – what was I supposed to do? I imagined I'd become disgusting to you. But now, when you talk about it, you turn it all around – as if it's my fault.

CELIA: That isn't how it was. We found something together
– we reached something, didn't we? I shared myself with
you – utterly – as I don't think I've ever done before. I
considered it a real accomplishment!

PIERRE: And afterwards you were sick in the toilet.

CELIA: Well, I don't understand that myself.

PIERRE: And you told me to get out.

CELIA: I asked you – I didn't tell. I said I needed a bit of time
alone. I only meant for you to go around the block. For a
walk. But you never came back. Or called to see if I was
alright.

Silence.

CELIA: The fact is, you were disappointed, Pierre. I wasn't
what you'd hoped I'd be.

PIERRE: That isn't true.

CELIA: Do you think a woman doesn't know every single
thought that goes through a man's head?

Silence.

PIERRE: Maybe I was disappointed. Flat. Like I'd been used
up. Playing a part I didn't comprehend. It wasn't me you
wanted. It was something else. An idea of someone else.

CELIA: Didn't I shout out your name? Remember how I
sobbed in your arms!

PIERRE: I didn't like that. What was there to cry about?

CELIA: God – it was as if a whole lifetime of shame and misery
and isolation was being lifted. I'd never been so liberated
– and so full of hope!

PIERRE: I'm sorry I didn't experience it like that. I felt
– trapped. Trapped in the old way, playing a part I never
chose for myself.

CELIA: Right.

Silence.

PIERRE: I'm sorry, Celia.

CELIA: For what?

PIERRE: For all the disappointment.

CELIA: That's far too vast a subject for you to grapple with.

PIERRE: There's no need to insult me.

CELIA: You call that an insult? That's not an insult! That's
a little song in the park. You coward. You liar. You
insinuating, spineless little boy – stealing biscuits from the
biscuit tin and then hiding away. Those are insults.

PIERRE: Why must you speak to me like this?

CELIA: You follow me around, go through my stuff, nose about
– like some dog. Then when you get at me at last, and have
satisfied yourself, you piss on me and slink off.

PIERRE: I'm not a dog.

CELIA: Aren't you? We make love – and then you leave,
without a word. For what? Some other bit of tail to sniff?
What's next for you, Pierre? Mandarin? Do you have a
pretty little Chinese pug all lined up?

PIERRE: Who are you – to talk to me about love!

CELIA: Why can't I?

PIERRE: You lie there like I'm raping you. All the time
shaking. Biting your lips. As if you're waiting for it to be
over. Sobbing. Clinging to me – like I'm some dead rock.
Trying not to be sick!

CELIA: Oh, stop it!

PIERRE: Then you shout 'come all over me', like it's
something disgusting you want to do to yourself. 'Come on

my breasts, come all over my mouth!' You cry out like a little girl – all the time using this stupid child's voice.

CELIA: Please stop!

PIERRE: You make me the little boy, stealing biscuits from the tin. But the child – that is you!

CELIA: Please!

PIERRE: You make me like rubbish. A criminal. Rapist! A savage!

CELIA: Well you are a savage, to speak to me like this!

PIERRE: But you are a nothing. Using me to make yourself look good. Without me, you don't even exist!

CELIA: Who taught you to speak to a woman like this?

PIERRE: Oh, be polite! Be polite! What's that about? You think I must be treated like an animal, insulted and spat at and kicked, and still I must have manners at the end of it? What do you expect? You people are all the same!

CELIA: What people is that?

PIERRE: White people!

CELIA: You're the racist – not me!

PIERRE: Black people can't be racists. We're the victims remember. We're the objects of racism.

CELIA: And will continue to be the objects as long as you get off on being the victims! You think we aren't all fucked up? We can all find our reasons to be fucked up.

PIERRE: Tell me – what did he do to you?

CELIA: Who?

PIERRE: You know exactly what I'm talking about!

CELIA: Get out!

PIERRE: Did you have sex? Did he fuck you? Did he come all over your face?

CELIA: Get out of my house!

PIERRE: He must have. How else can you explain yourself?

CELIA: Stop it!

PIERRE: Your brother is the rapist. But you make me into him. You keep him innocent. 'A good person,' you say. And you make me in the wrong. It's easy, isn't it? He's like you.

CELIA: He's nothing like me!

PIERRE: But me – I'm from somewhere else. It's easier to make me the animal and make him the good one. You want to fuck your brother, but that's too dark – so you choose to fuck me. You're like your mother! When you finish with us, what do you do? We must get out – get out of your houses!

CELIA: My brother is dead!

PIERRE: What?

CELIA: He's dead!

PIERRE: How dead? You said he was getting married!

CELIA: It was his funeral I was talking about – not his wedding.

PIERRE: What madness is this?

CELIA: He killed himself. Last month.

PIERRE: I don't believe you.

CELIA: He cut his wrists.

PIERRE: What?

CELIA: With a silver spoon!

PIERRE: You're playing your games with me.

CELIA: Am I? Perhaps I'm starting to express myself. It's what you wanted, isn't it? To see me for what I am. Well, I'm a liar and a thief. Alright? A murderer and a bitch. Are you satisfied?

PIERRE: No, I'm not satisfied. With you I'll never be satisfied. It's better if I go out and never come back. I don't even know why I come!

CELIA: Came! You came!

Silence.

CELIA: You know what? The thing you hate is not that you didn't enjoy it – it's that you did. You enjoyed pretending to rape me. You were as liberated by being an animal as I was. That's why you ran away. You were afraid of what you'd become.

PIERRE: Of what you wanted me to become.

CELIA: Yes – it was me. I showed you who you really are.

PIERRE: Well, it should be 'It was I' – not 'me'. You were the subject. I was the object.

Silence.

PIERRE: I think I've got as much out of these lessons as I need.

He takes out some money.

PIERRE: What's the expression? For services rendered?

He throws the money at her and walks out.

CELIA: Pierre!

Blackout.

Part Five

DEGREES OF UNCERTAINTY

It is six weeks later. The apartment is empty. It is no longer as neat as it was before. The front door is ajar. The daffodils are dead in their vase.

CELIA enters with a box. She is wearing the yellow dress. She looks pale and exhausted, her hair in disarray. She starts to pack some books in the box.

The phone rings.

CELIA: *Allô?* [Hello?]

Silence.

CELIA: Oh, hi Mum.

Silence.

CELIA: Yes, I'll be there.

> *The doorbell rings. CELIA doesn't move to open it. PIERRE pushes the door open and enters. He has a new, summery look about him.*

CELIA: I have to go. I'm in the middle of a lesson.

Silence.

CELIA: A boy.

Silence.

CELIA: He isn't at all attractive.

Silence.

CELIA: You too.

She hangs up.

PIERRE: Hello.

> *CELIA continues packing.*

PIERRE: What's happening?

CELIA: I didn't think you'd come.

PIERRE: Are you leaving?

CELIA: Yes.

PIERRE: Paris?

CELIA: Call it Paris if you like.

PIERRE: I see.

Silence.

PIERRE: Are you still angry with me?

CELIA: Call it angry if you like.

PIERRE: I've been feeling bad. About the way we left it. I'm glad you summoned me back. You call it 'unfinished business', not so?

CELIA: I don't think I have the words for it.

CELIA continues packing.

CELIA: You haven't even noticed.

PIERRE: What?

CELIA: I'm wearing the dress. Your yellow dress.

PIERRE: No, you –

He realises she is.

PIERRE: It looks different.

Silence.

CELIA: Perhaps I should have ironed it.

PIERRE: No. It's you who looks different.

CELIA: Thanks!

Silence.

PIERRE: You're still beautiful.

CELIA continues packing her books.

PIERRE: So what did you want? To say goodbye? To shout at me?

Silence.

PIERRE comes towards her, insinuating.

PIERRE: Or is it for something else? I've been missing you.

CELIA: The present perfect continuous. Good.

PIERRE: I went away. Back to Pouilly. I saw my old friend Etienne. The one who stole my girlfriend and kissed her under the tree. I thought I'd hit him – but all we did is stand by the river and share a cigarette. He tells me Elodie has married a middle-aged Belgian. He sells bicycle pumps. I must say – the gods are quick!

CELIA: I'm glad you've put all that behind you.

PIERRE: I can't tell you how much your lessons helped.

CELIA: Your English has certainly improved.

PIERRE: It's not only that. You gave me something. Call it my own tree to stand under. With my own girl.

CELIA: I see. You've met someone new. Does she speak Mandarin?

PIERRE: I haven't met anyone yet. But I am ready. Thanks to you.

CELIA: I'd have thought I would've put you off relationships.

PIERRE: No. *(He tries to joke.)* Only relationships with you!

Silence.

CELIA: You know, it was a cowardly thing to do. To change your number like that. But then you were always a bit – what's the word?

PIERRE: Elusive?

CELIA: Underhand.

Silence.

CELIA: Did it occur to you how I got your number?

PIERRE: I suppose you phoned the Sorbonne.

CELIA: The Post Office.

PIERRE: In Paris?

CELIA: In Pouilly-sur-Saone.

Silence.

CELIA: I spoke to a certain Madame de la Fontaine, I think it was. She hadn't a clue what I was talking about.

PIERRE: Why did you do that?

CELIA: She was insistent that there were no white families in Pouilly who had adopted a Congolese refugee. But when I described you, it all fell into place. She said she knew you well. She trotted out your parents' number right away.

PIERRE: She had no right!

CELIA: We had an interesting conversation. Your father and I. Would you like to know what he said?

PIERRE: Not really.

CELIA: I always knew something wasn't right. About your story. You simply didn't strike me as a refugee. As someone whose parents and siblings had been murdered, and thrown on a mountain of bodies to be burned. I could see you hadn't suffered. Not properly.

PIERRE: What do you know about what a person suffers?

CELIA: I told your father I was a journalist, wanting to write about refugees who had been adopted by French families. I said I believed he had an adopted son called Pierre.

PIERRE: I can't believe what I'm hearing!

CELIA: He told me that I'd made a mistake. You were his child. Or should I say 'arc'?

Silence.

CELIA: He sounded more than a little miffed when I asked if he was white.

PIERRE: Fuck you!

CELIA: He went on to confirm that you were born in France. And had never been adopted. You grew up in Pouilly. In a house by the river. The air thick with nightingales.

Silence.

CELIA: Why did you lie, Pierre? Did you want to make me feel sorry for you?

PIERRE: You have no business doing this!

CELIA: Or were you getting off yet again on being the victim? Cashing in on the suffering of others. What for – to look more appealing? Like a puppy in a shop window!

PIERRE: Who do you think you are?

CELIA: Making up stories like that! Tagging me along!

PIERRE: You told me to make something up. You said it doesn't have to literally be true. So that's what I did. Alright?

CELIA: From the start, all you wanted from me was sex!

PIERRE: I wanted so much more from you than that. And anyway – it wasn't a lie.

CELIA: What?

PIERRE: It was the truth!

Silence.

PIERRE: And it wasn't.

CELIA: It's little wonder you've never known how to express yourself – explain yourself. You're a mess!

PIERRE: It wasn't me from the Congo, alright? It was my parents.

Silence.

PIERRE: My father's from Lake Kivu, between Rwanda and the Congo. He moved to France when the country became Zaire. When the trouble started, he never went back. My mother – her people were from Butembo. She's the refugee. Those things that happened in the Congo. They would have happened to us, if my father hadn't left. That's the third conditional, isn't it?

CELIA: I – have no idea.

PIERRE: *Maman* [Mother] says I'm the lucky one. She watched her mother being raped and dumped in the river. Her father's genitals they threw in the yard for the dogs to eat.

Silence.

PIERRE: So you see, I was lying and I was not lying.

CELIA: I do see that.

Silence.

PIERRE: She also says, if something bad happens to one person, it happens to all of us. It's not the axe hitting the tree that reaches us, it's the echo.

Silence.

CELIA: I can't say I've ever felt that connection. When an axe hits a tree in the middle of a forest, do you feel it? You simply hear about it, don't you?

PIERRE: In Africa, you feel it. Maybe it's different here in Europe.

Silence.

PIERRE: You see, the trees have memory. Their roots take in the blood of the dead and carry it towards the light. They contain the memory of everything that has passed. When you hit one of the old trees with an axe, you are hitting yourself.

Silence.

CELIA: You really know how to take the wind out of a girl's sails, don't you?

PIERRE: I'm sorry I lied. I suppose I was trying to make myself more – exotic. I thought that's what you expected from me. Desired me to be. I wanted you to notice me – and be moved. To believe there was more to me than the nightingales.

CELIA: Oh, I do.

Silence.

PIERRE: Tell me your brother isn't dead.

CELIA: He isn't dead.

PIERRE: And is that the truth?

CELIA: He's very much alive. Living in Primrose Hill. Around the bend from my mother. And he's suddenly in love, apparently. Deliriously. To a redhead called Sophie.

PIERRE: When's the wedding?

CELIA: Next week. That's one of the reasons I'm leaving. I've finally agreed to go along. My mother tells me they're hiring a tent and having 'a bash' at Kenwood House.

PIERRE: So he's getting – better?

CELIA: Oh, there's nothing wrong with Olly. In fact, he's more than usually pleased with himself. Apparently this Sophie has enormous breasts.

PIERRE: But what about his thoughts?

CELIA: Which thoughts?

PIERRE: The intrusive ones. The ones that come from the outside.

CELIA: Oh those. Those are my thoughts. They come from me. From my inside.

PIERRE: From you?

CELIA: I'm the one who's sick.

Silence.

CELIA: I suppose you think me very strange.

PIERRE: It's one of the things I like about you.

CELIA: Nothing lasts for long, I always tell myself. We're sieves, unable to hold onto a mood, an emotion, even a conviction, for long. Everything that's poured into us dribbles out again. We're simply a place where things pass through, things we don't choose and whose final destination is unknown.

Silence.

PIERRE: When I saw you at the Sorbonne, you looked so perfect. I watched the way you greeted everyone. They all seemed to like you. The English girl passing through, leaving everything glowing slightly.

CELIA laughs bitterly.

PIERRE: I wondered what it would take to get your attention.

CELIA: You were enough to get my attention. As you were. From the moment you walked in with those stars in your hair.

They smile.

PIERRE: Did you tell my father about my lie?

CELIA: I said I must have made a mistake.

PIERRE: Thank you.

CELIA: I liked him. When we spoke.

PIERRE: You did?

CELIA: He wanted me to understand that he had achieved something – you.

Silence.

PIERRE: I don't want to leave you like this.

CELIA: You're leaving me. I'm like this.

CELIA picks up a pile of books and takes them to PIERRE.

CELIA: Here. Some of my favourite books. For you to take. As a gift. To keep up with the English.

She hands them over.

PIERRE: Novels?

He looks through the titles.

PIERRE: I prefer self-improvement books. Biographies. And histories. I can never find the time for stories that are made up. What's the point of that?

CELIA: Maybe we need to play around with the facts a little in order to make them bearable. It's why we dream. When we stop dreaming, we go insane.

PIERRE is still looking through the books.

PIERRE: So these are the ones you stole?

CELIA: Perhaps they're the ones I stole for you.

He laughs.

CELIA: You won't read them, will you?

PIERRE: I might.

CELIA: A thousand years of literacy – look where it's got us!

PIERRE stands.

CELIA: I wasn't very good at it, was I?

PIERRE: The sex?

CELIA: The teaching.

PIERRE: No, you weren't.

Silence.

PIERRE: You were too complicated about it.

CELIA: The teaching?

PIERRE: The sex.

They laugh.

PIERRE: The future tenses. We never got to them. You think there's time for one more lesson before I go?

CELIA: We may, we might. We can, we could. We should, we shall. We would, we will. These are all subjunctives. You can plot them on a graph. Each expresses a degree of uncertainty.

They regard each other.

CELIA: Or certainty.

Blackout.

The End.

Note on the author

Craig Higginson is a novelist, playwright, theatre director, dramaturge, editor and university lecturer. His first play, *Laughter in the Dark*, an adaptation of Nabokov's novel, opened at the Royal Shakespeare Company (RSC) in 2000. He later adapted it as a radio play for BBC Radio 3. It won the Sony Gold Award for Best Radio Drama in the UK for 2004-5. His first original play, *Dream of the Dog*, opened in Grahamstown and the Market Theatre in 2007 and was at the Hilton Festival in 2008. In 2010, *Dream of the Dog* opened at the Finborough in London, featuring Janet Suzman, and transferred to the Trafalgar Studios in London's West End. *Dream of the Dog* has been published by Wits Press and Oberon Books and is a university setwork. Craig's second original play, *The Girl in the Yellow Dress*, will open in Grahamstown in 2010, transfer to the Baxter Theatre (Cape Town), the Traverse Theatre (for the duration of the Edinburgh Festival), Live Theatre (Newcastle), the Citizens Theatre (Glasgow), the Stadsteater (Stockholm) and the Market Theatre (Johannesburg). Craig co-wrote *Truth in Translation* (Edinburgh Fringe First) and *Ten Bush*, both of which have toured widely internationally, and adapted and co-adapted several other works into plays for the Market Theatre. Craig's published novels include *The Hill* (2005, Jacana) and *Last Summer* (2010, Picador Africa). His next novel, *The Landscape Painter*, will appear in 2011 (Picador Africa).

Directing highlights include *Laughter in the Dark* (RSC, co-director), *Edward III* (RSC, staged reading), *Blood Wedding* (Pegasus Theatre, Oxford), *Grimm Tales* (Market Theatre), *Dream of the Dog* (Hilton Festival and SAFM), *The*

Perfect Circle (which he wrote for the Wits students) and *The Jungle Book* (Market Theatre).

Craig's writing and directing have been nominated for and won several awards in South Africa and the United Kingdom. The directors he has worked with include Barney Simon, Tim Supple, Michael Attenborough, David Farr, Maria Aitkin and Malcolm Purkey. Craig is the Literary Manager and dramaturge at the Market Theatre. He teaches playwriting at Wits. His plays and fiction are represented by PFD literary agency in London. In 2010, he will begin his PhD in Creative Writing at Wits.